Corruption at the Highest Levels of the U.S. Government Throughout History

Copyright Page

TITLE: Corruption at the Highest Levels of the U.S. Government Throughout History

1ST Edition

ISBN: 9798223161530

Table of Contents

Corruption at the Highest Levels of the U.S. Government Throughout History

By Roberto Miguel Rodriguez

Chapter 1: Corruption at the Highest Levels of the U.S. Government: Looking at Our History

The Origins of Government Corruption in the United States

Corruption has been a pervasive issue throughout the history of the United States government. This subchapter aims to delve into the origins of this deeply rooted problem, shedding light on the historical factors that have contributed to corruption at the highest levels of the U.S. government.

To understand the origins of government corruption, it is crucial to examine the early years of the U.S. government and the political scandals that occurred during this time. The formation of political parties, such as the Federalists and the Democratic-Republicans, created a competitive environment that often led to bribery and influence peddling. The infamous XYZ Affair and the Teapot Dome scandal are prime examples of early corruption that tainted the reputation of the U.S. government.

The role of money and lobbying has long been identified as a significant contributor to government corruption. As the country grew, so did the influence of wealthy individuals and corporations who sought to exert their power over the political process through financial contributions and lobbying efforts. This subchapter will explore the influence of money in politics and its detrimental impact on government ethics.

Furthermore, corruption within the executive branch, particularly presidential scandals, has had a profound effect on the perception of government integrity. From the Watergate scandal to more recent controversies like the Monica Lewinsky affair, examining these presidential scandals provides valuable insights into the nature of government corruption and its consequences.

Congress, as a legislative body, has not been immune to corruption either. Investigating bribery and influence peddling within Congress will shed light on the systemic issues that have allowed corruption to persist within this branch of government.

Additionally, this subchapter will explore corruption within law enforcement, the justice system, regulatory agencies, and the intelligence community. These sectors play a vital role in upholding the law and maintaining governmental integrity. However, instances of spying, surveillance scandals, and regulatory capture have demonstrated how corruption can infiltrate even these important institutions.

Examining corruption within the military and defense industry will further reveal the far-reaching consequences of government corruption. The intertwining of money, power, and national security has often resulted in unethical behavior and compromised decision-making.

Lastly, this subchapter will explore the role of journalism in uncovering government misconduct. The media has played a crucial role in exposing corruption throughout history, and understanding their impact is essential in the fight against government corruption.

By examining the origins of government corruption in the United States, this subchapter aims to provide historians and those interested in corruption at the highest levels of the U.S. government with a comprehensive understanding of the historical context and factors that have perpetuated this issue. Only through a thorough understanding of the past can we hope to address and combat corruption in the present and future.

Early Scandals: The Whiskey Ring and Credit Mobilier

In the annals of American history, corruption has been an enduring theme. From the birth of the nation, scandals and illicit activities have shadowed the highest levels of the U.S. government. Two infamous episodes, the Whiskey Ring and Credit Mobilier, serve as stark reminders of the challenges faced in combating corruption in the early years of the U.S. government.

The Whiskey Ring scandal rocked the Grant administration in the 1870s. At its core, the scandal involved a network of distillers, politicians, and government officials who colluded to evade taxes on whiskey production and distribution. This widespread conspiracy siphoned off millions of dollars from the federal treasury. The scandal implicated key figures within the Treasury Department, including the Secretary of the Treasury himself, who resigned amidst mounting evidence of his involvement. Investigations led to the prosecution and conviction of numerous individuals, including high-ranking government officials, tarnishing the reputation of the Grant administration.

Another scandal that sent shockwaves through the nation was the Credit Mobilier affair. This scandal exposed corruption within the construction of the transcontinental railroad in the 1860s. The Credit Mobilier construction company, owned by influential politicians and businessmen, engaged in fraudulent practices, overcharging the government for the railroad's construction. In a shocking twist, it was discovered that members of Congress were bribed with discounted company stock to ensure their silence and cooperation. This scandal not only highlighted the deep-seated corruption within Congress but also shed light on the pernicious role of money and lobbying in government affairs.

These early scandals underscore the need for eternal vigilance in combating corruption within the U.S. government. They reveal the insidious influence of money and the power of special interests in shaping policy decisions. From the executive branch to Congress, corruption took hold, eroding public trust in the institutions that were meant to serve the people.

As historians, it is our duty to study and analyze these early scandals, drawing lessons from the past to inform the present. By examining the systems and structures that allowed corruption to flourish, we can develop strategies to prevent future abuses of power. Moreover, we must recognize the crucial role played by the media and investigative journalism in uncovering government misconduct. The relentless pursuit of truth and transparency is essential in holding those in power accountable.

In conclusion, the Whiskey Ring and Credit Mobilier scandals serve as cautionary tales, reminding us of the enduring challenge of corruption at the highest levels of the U.S. government. By delving into these early scandals, we gain valuable insights into the history of political scandals and corruption and the complex interplay between money, power, and influence. Only through a comprehensive understanding of our past can we hope to build a more transparent and accountable future.

Corruption and Political Machines: Tammany Hall and Boss Tweed

Corruption has plagued governments throughout history, and the early years of the United States were no exception. One particular example that stands out is the notorious Tammany Hall and its leader, Boss Tweed. This subchapter delves into the dark underbelly of American politics during the 19th century, shedding light on the intricate web of corruption that entangled the highest levels of the U.S. government.

Tammany Hall, a powerful political machine in New York City, wielded immense influence over local politics for several decades. Led by the charismatic and manipulative Boss Tweed, the organization thrived on patronage, bribery, and cronyism. Through a system of favors and kickbacks, Tammany Hall controlled city contracts and appointments, ensuring its members remained in power and reaping substantial financial gains along the way.

Boss Tweed, a master of political manipulation, established an extensive network of loyal supporters, known as the Tweed Ring. This inner circle operated as a well-oiled machine, using their positions in government to embezzle millions of dollars from the city coffers. The scale of their corruption was staggering, with estimates suggesting that they siphoned off around $200 million (equivalent to billions today) through inflated contracts and fraudulent billing.

However, the reign of Tammany Hall and Boss Tweed could not last forever. Their corrupt practices eventually caught the attention of investigative journalists, most notably the political cartoonist Thomas Nast. Nast's scathing caricatures exposed the rampant corruption within Tammany Hall, effectively rallying public opinion against the corrupt political machine. In 1871, Tweed was arrested and eventually convicted on charges of fraud and larceny, marking the downfall of Tammany Hall.

The story of Tammany Hall and Boss Tweed serves as a cautionary tale, highlighting the dangers of unchecked political power and the devastating impact of corruption on democratic institutions. It underscores the importance of maintaining transparency, accountability, and a robust system of checks and balances within government.

By examining this chapter of American history, historians gain valuable insights into the roots of corruption in the U.S. government. It offers a window into the early years of political scandals and sheds light on the role of money and lobbying in corrupting the political process. Furthermore, it emphasizes the necessity of investigative journalism in exposing government misconduct and holding those in power accountable.

Overall, the story of Tammany Hall and Boss Tweed serves as a reminder that corruption has been a persistent challenge throughout American history. It urges historians to continue their exploration of corruption at the highest levels of the U.S. government, examining its impact on various branches and institutions. By learning from the past, we can strive to build a future where transparency and integrity prevail, ensuring a government that truly serves the interests of the people.

The Teapot Dome Scandal: A Turning Point in Government Corruption

In the annals of American government corruption, few scandals have left such an indelible mark as the Teapot Dome Scandal. This infamous episode, which unfolded in the early 1920s, revealed a shocking level of misconduct and kickbacks within the highest levels of the U.S. government. Historians consider it a turning point in the nation's battle against corruption, as it exposed the dark underbelly of political scandals and the pervasive influence of money and lobbying.

At the heart of the Teapot Dome Scandal was the illegal leasing of federal oil reserves in Wyoming and California. These reserves were intended for use by the U.S. Navy, but under the administration of President Warren G. Harding, they were secretly transferred to private companies. The man responsible for orchestrating this illicit scheme was Albert B. Fall, the Secretary of the Interior.

Fall's actions were driven by greed and a desire for personal enrichment. In exchange for granting oil leases to private companies, he received substantial bribes and kickbacks. This blatant abuse of power and betrayal of public trust sent shockwaves through the nation and sparked widespread outrage.

The Teapot Dome Scandal not only revealed the extent of corruption within the executive branch but also shed light on the role of money and lobbying in perpetuating government misconduct. It exposed the dangerous intersection of business interests and political power, where influential individuals could use their financial clout to manipulate government decisions for personal gain.

Furthermore, the scandal prompted a deeper examination of corruption within Congress, as investigations revealed the involvement of several members in the bribery and influence peddling surrounding the Teapot Dome leases. It also raised questions about the integrity of law enforcement and the justice system, as certain individuals managed to evade punishment or receive lenient sentences due to their connections and influence.

The impact of the Teapot Dome Scandal extended beyond the immediate consequences for those involved. It highlighted the need for comprehensive campaign finance reform to curb the influence of money in politics. It also underscored the crucial role of journalism in uncovering government misconduct, as investigative reporters played a vital role in exposing the scandal and holding corrupt officials accountable.

In the decades that followed, the Teapot Dome Scandal served as a cautionary tale and a catalyst for reform. It demonstrated the importance of transparency, accountability, and ethical governance in preserving the integrity of the U.S. government. While corruption has persisted throughout history, the Teapot Dome Scandal remains a milestone in the ongoing fight against government misconduct, reminding us of the need to remain vigilant and uphold the principles upon which our democracy was built.

Chapter 2: Political scandals and corruption in the early years of the U.S. government

The XYZ Affair: Foreign Intrigue and Political Corruption

In the annals of American history, few events have captured the imagination and exposed the underbelly of political corruption quite like the XYZ Affair. Spanning the late 18th century, this scandalous episode sheds light on the intricate web of foreign intrigue and political corruption that plagued the early years of the U.S. government.

The XYZ Affair unfolded against the backdrop of strained relations between the United States and France. In an attempt to broker peace and prevent a full-scale war, President John Adams dispatched a diplomatic mission to Paris in 1797. Little did he know that this mission would unravel a vast network of bribery, influence peddling, and manipulation that reached into the highest levels of the French government.

Upon their arrival in Paris, the American diplomats were met with a surprising demand from French officials - a hefty bribe simply to engage in diplomatic negotiations. Shocked and appalled, the Americans refused to comply, and the scandal erupted into the public consciousness.

Dubbed the XYZ Affair after the code names given to the French intermediaries involved, this incident exposed the corrupt underbelly of international diplomacy. It revealed how personal gain and financial interests could supersede the pursuit of peace, tarnishing the reputations of both American and French officials.

The XYZ Affair also highlighted the role of money and lobbying in government corruption. It brought into sharp focus the power of wealthy individuals and special interest groups to influence decision-making and undermine the integrity of the political process. This scandal served as a wake-up call for the young nation, prompting a reevaluation of the role of money in politics and the need for transparency in government affairs.

Furthermore, the XYZ Affair underscored the vulnerability of the executive branch to corrupt practices. It emphasized the importance of ethical leadership and the need for presidents to maintain the highest standards of integrity. This scandal prompted a thorough examination of presidential conduct and set the stage for future investigations into executive branch corruption.

For historians and those interested in the history of corruption in the highest levels of the U.S. government, the XYZ Affair remains a pivotal moment. It serves as a cautionary tale, reminding us of the ever-present dangers of foreign intrigue and political corruption. By studying this dark chapter in our history, we gain valuable insights into the lasting impact of these issues on American democracy and the ongoing struggle to maintain ethical governance.

The Burr-Hamilton Duel: Personal Rivalries and Political Consequences

In the annals of American history, few events have captured the imagination and intrigue of historians quite like the Burr-Hamilton Duel. This infamous confrontation between political rivals Aaron Burr and Alexander Hamilton not only ended one man's life but also had far-reaching consequences for the nascent U.S. government.

The duel itself was the culmination of a long-standing personal rivalry between Burr and Hamilton. Both men were prominent figures in the early years of the United States, with Burr serving as Vice President and Hamilton as Secretary of the Treasury. Their differing political ideologies, combined with a deep-seated animosity, set the stage for a deadly clash.

On that fateful day in July 1804, Hamilton and Burr met on the dueling grounds in Weehawken, New Jersey. The reasons behind their duel remain shrouded in mystery, but it is widely believed that the final straw was Hamilton's public disparagement of Burr's character during the contentious 1804 New York gubernatorial election.

Hamilton, a renowned orator and political strategist, had a formidable reputation. However, his decision to engage in a duel ultimately proved fatal. As the two men raised their pistols, Hamilton fired into the air, adhering to a personal code of honor. Burr, on the other hand, aimed directly at his opponent, mortally wounding Hamilton.

The immediate consequences of the duel were profound. Hamilton's death sent shockwaves through the political landscape, leaving a void in the Federalist Party, and effectively ending Burr's political career. Burr would later face treason charges for his alleged involvement in a conspiracy to establish an independent nation in the American West.

Beyond the personal ramifications, the Burr-Hamilton Duel highlighted the dangers of personal rivalries and the fragility of the early U.S. government. The duel underscored the deep divisions within the nation and the potential for violence to resolve political disputes. It also shed light on the influence of money and lobbying in government corruption, as Burr's alleged involvement in land speculation schemes and his bid for power further tainted his reputation.

For historians studying corruption at the highest levels of the U.S. government, the Burr-Hamilton Duel serves as a cautionary tale. It reminds us of the role personal rivalries can play in shaping political outcomes and the far-reaching consequences of unchecked ambition. By examining this pivotal moment in American history, we gain valuable insights into the complex dynamics of corruption and its impact on the early years of the U.S. government.

The Crédit Mobilier Scandal: Corruption and the Railroad Industry

Introduction:

In the annals of American history, corruption has plagued the highest levels of government since its inception. One such scandal that exposed the dark underbelly of the U.S. government was the Crédit Mobilier scandal. This shocking episode unfolded within the railroad industry, revealing a web of deceit, bribery, and influence peddling that tainted the very fabric of American democracy.

The Birth of Crédit Mobilier:

The Crédit Mobilier was a construction company formed during the 1860s, tasked with building the First Transcontinental Railroad. However, it soon became clear that this seemingly noble venture was a front for a nefarious scheme. The company's executives, including high-ranking government officials, embarked on a path of corruption and self-enrichment that would shake the nation to its core.

Bribery and Influence Peddling:

At the heart of the scandal lay a complex web of bribery and influence peddling. The Crédit Mobilier executives sought to secure exorbitant profits by overcharging the government for their construction services. To ensure their scheme remained intact, they lavishly bribed members of Congress, including influential figures such as Vice President Schuyler Colfax. These politicians, entrusted with safeguarding the nation's interests, shamelessly succumbed to the allure of wealth and power.

The Fallout and Public Outrage:

As news of the scandal broke, the American public was left in shock and dismay. The Crédit Mobilier scandal symbolized a betrayal of trust and the erosion of democratic values. The public's outrage was palpable, leading to widespread demands for justice and reform.

Investigations and Repercussions:

The scandal triggered a series of investigations, both within Congress and by the media, determined to uncover the full extent of the corruption. Congressional hearings shed light on the deep-rooted systemic issues that allowed such corruption to thrive within the railroad industry. The fallout from the scandal resulted in the censure of several high-ranking politicians, tarnishing their legacies forever.

Legacy and Lessons Learned:

The Crédit Mobilier scandal served as a wake-up call for the American people and the government. It exposed the dangerous nexus between money, lobbying, and corruption in the halls of power. The scandal prompted reforms aimed at curbing the influence of money in politics, ultimately leading to the passage of legislation to regulate campaign finance and lobbying activities.

Conclusion:

The Crédit Mobilier scandal stands as a stark reminder of the corrosive nature of corruption within the U.S. government. It serves as a cautionary tale for future generations, reminding us of the constant vigilance required to safeguard democratic institutions from the clutches of greed and self-interest. As historians, we must continue to shine a light on such scandals, ensuring that the lessons learned from the past guide us toward a more transparent and accountable future.

The Tweed Ring: A Dark Era of Political Corruption in New York

In the annals of American political corruption, few periods are as notorious and brazen as the era of the Tweed Ring in New York City. This dark chapter in our nation's history, marked by rampant bribery, embezzlement, and fraud, serves as a stark reminder of the depths to which government officials can sink when unchecked by a vigilant citizenry.

Led by the infamous William M. Tweed, better known as "Boss Tweed," the Tweed Ring operated with impunity throughout the 1860s and early 1870s. Tweed, a Democratic politician, began his rise to power as a member of the New York City Board of Supervisors. Through a web of bribery, kickbacks, and rigged elections, he soon consolidated his control over the city's government.

Under the Tweed Ring's rule, corruption infected nearly every aspect of New York City politics. Public funds were siphoned off into the pockets of Tweed and his cronies, leading to exorbitant expenditures on public projects that benefited them personally. The most infamous example of this was the construction of the New York County Courthouse, which ended up costing taxpayers an astronomical sum, with much of the money lining the pockets of the Tweed Ring.

The Tweed Ring's influence extended far beyond the city government. They leveraged their ill-gotten wealth to control the state legislature and the judiciary, ensuring that anyone who dared to challenge their authority would face swift retribution. Newspapers that dared to investigate or criticize the Tweed Ring were bought off or silenced through intimidation.

It was not until the investigative journalism of the renowned cartoonist Thomas Nast and the reporting of The New York Times that the full extent of the Tweed Ring's corruption was exposed. Nast's political cartoons, which vividly depicted Tweed as a bloated and corrupt figure, played a crucial role in galvanizing public opinion against the Ring.

Ultimately, Tweed was brought down through a combination of media scrutiny, citizen activism, and the efforts of a newly appointed district attorney, Samuel Tilden. Tweed was tried and convicted for his crimes, but the damage had already been done. The Tweed Ring had left an indelible mark on New York City, tarnishing the reputation of its government and reinforcing public skepticism towards politicians.

The legacy of the Tweed Ring serves as a cautionary tale for all who study corruption in the highest levels of the U.S. government. It demonstrates the ease with which power can be abused and the need for constant vigilance to ensure that those in positions of authority are held accountable. Only by understanding and learning from the mistakes of the past can we hope to prevent such dark eras from recurring in our nation's history.

Chapter 3: The role of money and lobbying in government corruption

The Influence of Big Money: Campaign Contributions and Corruption

Throughout history, the United States government has been plagued by corruption at the highest levels. One of the key factors contributing to this corruption is the influence of big money in the form of campaign contributions. This subchapter will delve into the intricate relationship between campaign contributions and corruption, shedding light on the dark shadows that often cloud our government.

Campaign contributions, although a necessary part of the political process, have long been a source of concern for historians and scholars. The sheer amount of money flowing into political campaigns raises questions about the potential for corruption. When wealthy individuals and special interest groups donate large sums of money to politicians, there is a natural inclination for those politicians to favor their benefactors. This quid pro quo arrangement undermines the democratic principles on which our government was founded.

Political scandals and corruption in the early years of the U.S. government serve as a testament to the long-standing issue of money's influence. From the infamous Teapot Dome scandal of the 1920s to the Watergate scandal of the 1970s, money has played a central role in corrupting our government officials. These historical examples provide valuable insights into the ways in which campaign contributions can lead to unethical behavior and abuse of power.

Furthermore, the role of money and lobbying in government corruption cannot be ignored. Lobbyists, often representing powerful interest groups, use their financial resources to gain access to politicians and push for policies that benefit their clients. This system of legalized bribery erodes the integrity of our government and undermines the voices of ordinary citizens.

Corruption is not limited to a single branch of government. The executive branch has seen its fair share of presidential scandals, where campaign contributions have been at the heart of illegal activities. From the infamous "Cash for Pardons" scandal under President Clinton to the more recent allegations of foreign influence in the 2016 election, the impact of big money on corruption within the executive branch cannot be underestimated.

Similarly, corruption within Congress has been a persistent problem. Investigating bribery and influence peddling reveals the extent to which campaign contributions can sway legislative decisions. Regulatory agencies, law enforcement, and even the justice system have also been tainted by corruption, often fueled by the influence of money.

The impact of campaign finance on government corruption cannot be overstated. The Supreme Court's Citizens United decision in 2010 opened the floodgates for unlimited corporate spending in political campaigns. This decision has further entrenched the influence of big money in our political system, making it even more difficult to address the issue of corruption.

As historians, it is crucial to examine and understand the deep-rooted connection between campaign contributions and corruption. By uncovering the ways in which money has influenced our government throughout history, we can work towards creating a more transparent and accountable system. Only by shining a light on these shadows can we hope to restore the integrity of our government and ensure a truly democratic society.

Lobbying and the Corruption of Legislative Decision-Making

In the realm of government corruption, few issues are as pervasive and insidious as the influence of lobbying on legislative decision-making. Throughout the history of the United States, the intertwining of money, power, and politics has created a breeding ground for corruption at the highest levels of government. This subchapter will delve into the intricate web of lobbying and its detrimental effects on the legislative process.

From the early years of the U.S. government, political scandals and corruption have plagued the nation. However, it is the role of money and lobbying that has accelerated the corruption to unprecedented levels. Lobbyists, representing powerful interest groups and corporations, have become masters of manipulation within the legislative arena. Through campaign contributions, lavish gifts, and promises of future employment, lobbyists have effectively corrupted the decision-making process.

The executive branch has not been immune to corruption, with numerous presidential scandals staining the pages of history. From the Teapot Dome scandal to Watergate, the influence of money and lobbying has seeped into the highest office of the land, compromising the integrity of the presidency.

Similarly, corruption within Congress has been a persistent issue. Bribery and influence peddling have become commonplace, with lobbyists using their financial prowess to sway lawmakers in their favor. The result is a legislative body that caters to the interests of the highest bidder, rather than the needs and desires of the American people.

Corruption is not limited to the legislative and executive branches. The justice system, regulatory agencies, intelligence community, military, and even the media have all been implicated in various corruption scandals throughout history. This subchapter will explore the extent of corruption within these institutions and the role that lobbying and money play in perpetuating the misconduct.

Furthermore, the impact of campaign finance on government corruption cannot be understated. The influx of money into political campaigns has created a system in which elected officials are indebted to their donors, rather than the constituents they serve. This subchapter will examine the detrimental effects of campaign finance on the integrity of the legislative process.

Ultimately, lobbying and the corruption of legislative decision-making have become deeply entrenched within the fabric of the U.S. government. To fully understand the extent of corruption at the highest levels, it is essential to examine the role of money, power, and lobbying in shaping our nation's history. By shedding light on this pervasive issue, we can begin to unravel the shadows of corruption and work towards a more transparent and accountable government.

The Rise of Super PACs: Money, Power, and Corruption in Politics

In the world of American politics, the rise of Super Political Action Committees (Super PACs) has been nothing short of a game-changer. These independent expenditure-only committees, which came into existence after the infamous Citizens United Supreme Court ruling in 2010, have transformed the landscape of campaign finance and exerted a significant influence on the political process.

Super PACs are allowed to raise and spend unlimited amounts of money, thanks to the notion that money is a form of expression protected by the First Amendment. This newfound power has unleashed a flood of cash into the political arena, enabling wealthy individuals, corporations, and special interest groups to exert their influence on the electoral process like never before.

With this surge in financial power comes the inevitable question of corruption. Critics argue that the presence of Super PACs has created a breeding ground for political corruption, as the prospects of receiving substantial campaign contributions can sway politicians' decisions and priorities. The concern is that elected officials may become indebted to their wealthy donors, compromising the integrity of governance and undermining the democratic process.

Furthermore, the lack of transparency surrounding Super PACs exacerbates these concerns. Unlike traditional political action committees, Super PACs are not required to disclose their donors until after an election, allowing for potential hidden agendas and undisclosed influences to shape political outcomes. This opacity fuels suspicions of corruption and erodes public trust in the political system.

The influence of Super PACs is particularly evident in the executive branch, where presidential scandals have become synonymous with corruption. From Watergate to the Iran-Contra affair, these scandals have often involved the misuse of funds, influence peddling, and illicit campaign contributions. The rise of Super PACs has only amplified these issues, providing a powerful tool for those aiming to influence presidential decision-making and potentially leading to further corruption.

Congress, too, has not been immune to the corrosive effects of money and lobbying. Bribery and influence peddling have plagued the halls of power throughout history, and the advent of Super PACs has only intensified these problems. The ability to pour unlimited funds into political campaigns allows wealthy individuals and interest groups to buy access and favors, perpetuating a cycle of corruption that undermines the very foundations of democracy.

Moreover, corruption extends beyond the political realm, infiltrating law enforcement agencies, the justice system, regulatory bodies, the intelligence community, the military, and even the media. Scandals involving these institutions have exposed the deep-rooted nature of corruption in the highest levels of the U.S. government, highlighting the need for continued scrutiny and investigation.

Ultimately, the rise of Super PACs and the confluence of money, power, and corruption in politics demand our attention as historians. By examining the historical context, the role of campaign finance, and the impact on various government institutions, we can better understand the challenges we face today. Only through a comprehensive understanding of these issues can we hope to address and rectify the corruption that undermines the integrity and effectiveness of our democratic system.

The Revolving Door: Corruption and the Influence of Corporate Lobbyists

Throughout the pages of history, corruption has woven its way into the highest levels of the U.S. government. In this subchapter, we delve into a particularly insidious form of corruption - the revolving door between the government and corporate lobbyists. This phenomenon exposes the deep-rooted influence of money and special interests in shaping policy decisions and undermining the integrity of our democratic system.

Corporate lobbyists, representing the interests of powerful industries, have long sought to influence legislation and regulations that favor their clients. This revolving door refers to the seamless movement of individuals between positions in the government and lucrative jobs in the private sector. The result is a toxic blend of corporate influence and government power, where the lines between public service and private gain become increasingly blurred.

The allure of these lucrative job opportunities often tempts government officials to prioritize the interests of corporations over those of the general public. This compromises the integrity of our democratic institutions, as policies are crafted to benefit the few rather than the many. The revolving door creates a system in which corporate interests hold disproportionate power, undermining the principles of equality and fairness upon which our nation was founded.

This subchapter examines various historical examples of this revolving door phenomenon. We explore how corporate lobbyists have infiltrated the executive branch, influencing presidential decisions and scandalizing administrations. We delve into Congress, where bribery and influence peddling have tainted the legislative process, highlighting the need for comprehensive campaign finance reform.

Furthermore, we investigate corruption within regulatory agencies, where industry insiders often dictate regulations that favor their own interests. The impact of campaign finance on government corruption is also analyzed, shedding light on the role of money in perpetuating this vicious cycle.

Finally, we explore the intersection of corruption, the media, and journalism. Investigative journalists have played a crucial role in uncovering government misconduct and shining a light on the influence of corporate lobbyists. By examining their work, we gain insight into the vital role of a free press in safeguarding our democracy.

In conclusion, the revolving door between the government and corporate lobbyists is a grave concern that threatens the very fabric of our democracy. By understanding its historical roots and examining its impact on various branches of government and sectors of society, we can begin to address this pervasive issue and strive for a government that truly represents the interests of the people.

Chapter 4: Corruption in the executive branch: examining presidential scandals

Watergate: The Scandal that Shook the Nation

The Watergate scandal is undoubtedly one of the most significant political scandals in the history of the United States. It not only exposed high-level corruption within the government but also dealt a severe blow to the public's trust in their elected officials. In this subchapter, we will delve into the details of the Watergate scandal, its aftermath, and the lasting impact it had on American politics.

The Watergate scandal began on June 17, 1972, when five men were arrested for breaking into the Democratic National Committee headquarters at the Watergate complex in Washington, D.C. Initially regarded as a minor incident, it soon unraveled into a web of political espionage and illegal activities orchestrated by members of President Richard Nixon's administration.

As investigations continued, it became clear that the break-in was just the tip of the iceberg. The scandal eventually led to the revelation of a secret White House taping system, which recorded conversations between Nixon and his advisors. These tapes would prove to be crucial evidence of Nixon's involvement in the cover-up of the break-in and subsequent illegal activities.

The Watergate scandal not only exposed the corruption within the executive branch but also highlighted the role of money and lobbying in government corruption. It revealed the extent to which Nixon's reelection campaign had relied on illegal campaign contributions and demonstrated the influence of money in politics.

Moreover, the scandal exposed the abuse of power and obstruction of justice by high-ranking government officials, including the President himself. The subsequent investigation by the Congress, media, and the justice system revealed a systemic problem of corruption within regulatory agencies, law enforcement, and the intelligence community.

The impact of the Watergate scandal was profound. It led to President Nixon's resignation in 1974, making him the first and only U.S. president to resign from office. The scandal also triggered significant reforms in campaign finance laws and ethics regulations, aiming to prevent similar abuses of power in the future.

The Watergate scandal shook the nation to its core, leaving a lasting impact on American politics and society. It taught the American people valuable lessons about the importance of transparency, accountability, and the need to safeguard the integrity of their government. The investigative journalism that uncovered the scandal also highlighted the crucial role of the media in exposing government misconduct, inspiring a new era of investigative reporting.

In conclusion, the Watergate scandal serves as a stark reminder of the dangers of unchecked government power and the need for constant vigilance against corruption at the highest levels of the U.S. government. Its enduring legacy continues to shape discussions on political scandals, government accountability, and the role of journalism in uncovering government misconduct.

Iran-Contra Affair: Covert Operations and Government Corruption

The Iran-Contra Affair stands as one of the most notorious political scandals in the history of the United States. It revealed a web of covert operations, government corruption, and the erosion of democratic principles. This subchapter delves into the intricacies and implications of this scandal, shedding light on the dark underbelly of the U.S. government.

The Iran-Contra Affair emerged in the 1980s during the Reagan administration. It involved the clandestine sale of weapons to Iran, despite an arms embargo, in exchange for the release of American hostages held in Lebanon. The proceeds from these sales were then funneled to fund the Contras, an anti-communist rebel group in Nicaragua, despite a congressional ban on such support. This covert operation was conducted by high-ranking officials within the executive branch, with the knowledge and approval of President Ronald Reagan.

At its core, the Iran-Contra Affair exposed a blatant disregard for the rule of law and a culture of corruption within the highest levels of the U.S. government. The Reagan administration sought to pursue its foreign policy objectives outside the bounds of congressional oversight and public scrutiny. This flagrant abuse of power undermined the very foundations of democracy and eroded public trust.

The repercussions of the Iran-Contra Affair were far-reaching. It not only tarnished the reputation of the Reagan administration but also raised questions about the integrity of the U.S. government as a whole. It highlighted the dangers of unchecked executive power and the potential for corruption in covert operations.

This subchapter aims to provide historians with a comprehensive analysis of the Iran-Contra Affair, exploring the intricate web of covert operations, government corruption, and the erosion of democratic principles that characterized this scandal. By examining the motivations, actors, and consequences of this affair, historians can gain a deeper understanding of the challenges posed by corruption at the highest levels of the U.S. government.

By studying the Iran-Contra Affair, historians can draw parallels and lessons from this dark chapter in American history. It serves as a cautionary tale, underscoring the importance of accountability, transparency, and the preservation of democratic institutions. As we navigate the present-day landscape of political scandals and corruption, the lessons learned from the Iran-Contra Affair remain as relevant as ever.

Bill Clinton's Impeachment: The Monica Lewinsky Scandal

The Monica Lewinsky scandal remains one of the most infamous and widely discussed political scandals in the history of the United States. It shook the nation to its core and forever tarnished the legacy of President Bill Clinton. This subchapter delves into the details of this scandal, exploring its significance in the context of corruption at the highest levels of the U.S. government.

The scandal erupted in 1998 when allegations of President Clinton's affair with a young White House intern named Monica Lewinsky became public. The revelation sent shockwaves throughout the nation and led to a lengthy and contentious impeachment process. The scandal exposed the dark underbelly of corruption within the executive branch and raised serious questions about the integrity of the presidency.

At the heart of the scandal was the abuse of power and the manipulation of the justice system. President Clinton, facing allegations of perjury and obstruction of justice, engaged in a series of evasive tactics and misleading statements to protect his reputation. This blatant disregard for the law and the Constitution highlighted the extent to which corruption had infiltrated the highest levels of government.

The Lewinsky scandal also shed light on the role of money and lobbying in government corruption. It revealed how individuals with wealth and influence could exploit their connections to gain favor and access to the corridors of power. The scandal exposed the vulnerability of the U.S. political system to the influence of money, highlighting the need for campaign finance reform and stricter regulations on lobbying.

Furthermore, the scandal had a profound impact on the media landscape and the role of journalism in exposing government misconduct. The relentless pursuit of truth by investigative journalists, such as Linda Tripp, helped uncover the scandal and hold President Clinton accountable. It underscored the crucial role of the media in uncovering corruption and serving as a watchdog for democracy.

In conclusion, the Monica Lewinsky scandal serves as a stark reminder of the extent of corruption at the highest levels of the U.S. government. It exposed the abuse of power, the influence of money, and the erosion of trust in the presidency. By examining this scandal, historians can gain valuable insights into the challenges of combating corruption and upholding the principles of democracy.

The Plame Affair: Political Vendettas and Government Secrecy

In the annals of political scandals and government corruption, few incidents have captured the attention of the American public like the Plame Affair. This subchapter delves deep into the intricate web of deception, revenge, and government secrecy that unfolded during this notorious episode.

The Plame Affair refers to the leak of Valerie Plame's covert identity as a CIA operative by members of the U.S. government in 2003. Plame, married to former U.S. Ambassador Joseph Wilson, became embroiled in a political firestorm when her husband publicly criticized the Bush administration's justification for the Iraq War. In an act of retribution, high-ranking officials within the government exposed Plame's secret role, endangering her life and jeopardizing national security.

This scandal raises critical questions about the abuse of power and the lengths some politicians are willing to go to silence dissent and protect their own interests. It also brings to light the pervasive culture of secrecy that permeates the highest levels of the U.S. government, allowing corruption to fester unchecked.

Examining the Plame Affair through the lens of corruption at the highest levels of the U.S. government offers valuable insights into the inner workings of political vendettas and the erosion of transparency. It also underscores the importance of whistleblowing and the role it plays in uncovering government misconduct.

This subchapter will explore the intricate dynamics of the Plame Affair, shedding light on the individuals involved, their motivations, and the consequences of their actions. It will delve into the ethical implications of government secrecy and its impact on democracy and public trust. Additionally, it will analyze the legal and political fallout from this scandal and its lasting effects on the intelligence community.

By examining the Plame Affair, historians can gain a deeper understanding of the patterns of corruption and abuse of power that have plagued the U.S. government throughout history. This subchapter serves as a reminder that vigilance and transparency are essential in holding our leaders accountable and preserving the integrity of our democratic institutions. Only by uncovering the shadows of corruption can we strive for a more transparent and accountable government for future generations.

Chapter 5: Corruption in Congress: investigating bribery and influence peddling

Abscam: The FBI Sting Operation that Exposed Congressional Corruption

In the annals of U.S. history, corruption has often reared its ugly head within the highest levels of government. One such scandal that shook the nation was Abscam, an FBI sting operation that exposed the depths of congressional corruption in the late 1970s and early 1980s. This subchapter delves into the intricate details of Abscam, shedding light on the extent of the bribery and influence peddling that plagued the halls of Congress.

Abscam, short for "Arab scam," was an undercover operation devised by the FBI to uncover political corruption. It involved FBI agents masquerading as wealthy Arab businessmen seeking favors from elected officials. Their aim was to expose the vulnerability of lawmakers to monetary temptations and highlight the systemic flaws that allowed such corruption to persist.

The operation initially targeted members of Congress who were suspected of accepting bribes in exchange for legislative favors. As the investigation progressed, it became evident that the corruption extended beyond the legislative branch, reaching into executive agencies, law enforcement, and regulatory bodies. This revelation shook the nation's faith in the integrity of its government and prompted a thorough reevaluation of the systems in place to prevent such abuses of power.

One of the key findings of Abscam was the role of money and lobbying in government corruption. The investigation uncovered a web of lobbyists and middlemen who acted as conduits between wealthy individuals seeking favors and lawmakers willing to oblige for a price. This revelation highlighted the need for comprehensive campaign finance reform and stricter regulations on lobbying activities.

Abscam also exposed the dark underbelly of congressional influence peddling. Elected officials were caught on tape accepting cash bribes in exchange for political favors, thereby compromising the democratic process. The scandal led to a series of high-profile prosecutions, including the conviction of several congressmen and senators, further tarnishing the reputation of the U.S. government.

The impact of Abscam reverberated across various sectors, including the intelligence community, the military, and the media. It highlighted the potential for corruption within these institutions and underscored the importance of rigorous oversight and accountability.

In conclusion, Abscam stands as a testament to the enduring struggle against corruption at the highest levels of the U.S. government. This chapter provides a comprehensive examination of this infamous scandal, shedding light on its far-reaching consequences and serving as a cautionary tale for future generations. By understanding the history of corruption in our government, we can strive to build a more transparent and accountable democracy for all.

The Jack Abramoff Scandal: Lobbyists, Bribes, and Political Influence

The Jack Abramoff scandal is a prime example of the far-reaching consequences of corruption and the influence of money in the U.S. government. This chapter delves into the intricate details of the scandal, shedding light on the web of lobbyists, bribes, and political influence that tainted the highest levels of power.

Jack Abramoff, a prominent lobbyist, was once considered one of the most powerful individuals in Washington, D.C. His vast network of connections allowed him to wield significant influence over lawmakers and government officials. However, it was his unethical practices and pursuit of personal gain that ultimately led to his downfall.

The scandal erupted in the mid-2000s when Abramoff's corrupt activities were exposed to the public. It was revealed that he had been involved in a series of illegal activities, including bribery, fraud, and influence peddling. Abramoff and his associates had exploited their relationships with lawmakers, using lavish gifts, luxury trips, and campaign contributions to manipulate the political process in their favor.

One of the most shocking aspects of the scandal was the extent of Abramoff's connections within the U.S. government. He had cultivated relationships with high-ranking officials, including members of Congress and even White House officials. This allowed him to gain unprecedented access and influence over key decision-making processes, often to the detriment of public interest.

The scandal also exposed the dark underbelly of the lobbying industry. It highlighted how money and special interests can easily corrupt the political system, undermining the democratic principles upon which the United States was founded. The revelation of Abramoff's actions sparked widespread outrage and led to calls for reform in lobbying regulations and campaign finance laws.

This subchapter not only examines the intricacies of the Jack Abramoff scandal but also delves into the broader issue of corruption within the U.S. government. It explores the historical context of political scandals and corruption, tracing their roots back to the early years of the country. It also analyzes the role of money and lobbying in perpetuating government corruption, examining the impact of campaign finance on the integrity of the political process.

By shedding light on the Jack Abramoff scandal, this subchapter aims to provide historians and those interested in government corruption with a comprehensive understanding of the far-reaching consequences of unethical practices. It serves as a stark reminder of the importance of transparency, accountability, and ethical behavior in ensuring the integrity of the U.S. government and upholding the democratic values upon which the nation was built.

The Duke Cunningham Scandal: Corruption and Defense Contracts

In the annals of American political scandals, the Duke Cunningham scandal stands out as a stark reminder of the rampant corruption that has plagued the highest levels of the U.S. government throughout history. This subchapter delves into the sordid details of this scandal, shedding light on the intricate web of corruption and the insidious influence of defense contracts.

Randy "Duke" Cunningham, a former U.S. Navy fighter pilot turned Congressman, rose to prominence as a decorated war hero. However, behind his patriotic facade lay a web of deceit and corruption that would eventually unravel and send shockwaves through the nation. Cunningham's downfall began when he used his position on the Defense Appropriations Subcommittee to secure lucrative defense contracts for his friends and political allies.

The scandal came to light in 2005 when federal investigators discovered that Cunningham had received over $2.4 million in bribes from defense contractors in exchange for steering government contracts their way. These contractors showered him with lavish gifts, including a Rolls-Royce, a luxury yacht, and even a Persian rug worth tens of thousands of dollars. Cunningham's greed knew no bounds, as he shamelessly exploited his position for personal gain.

The Duke Cunningham scandal exposed the dark underbelly of corruption within the defense industry and highlighted the role of money and lobbying in perpetuating this corruption. It revealed how defense contractors, driven by profit, were willing to go to great lengths to secure lucrative government contracts, even resorting to bribing elected officials. This scandal served as a wake-up call, forcing lawmakers and the public alike to confront the systemic issues that allowed such corruption to fester within the government.

The impact of the Duke Cunningham scandal reverberated beyond the defense industry, shaking the core of the U.S. government. It sparked a renewed interest in investigating corruption within the executive branch, shedding light on other presidential scandals throughout history. It also exposed the deep-seated corruption within Congress, as lawmakers were implicated in bribery and influence peddling.

Furthermore, the Duke Cunningham scandal prompted a reevaluation of campaign finance laws and the role of money in corrupting the political process. It exposed the vulnerabilities within regulatory agencies and raised questions about the integrity of the justice system and law enforcement in combating government misconduct.

The media played a crucial role in uncovering the Duke Cunningham scandal, highlighting the vital role of journalism in exposing government corruption. It served as a stark reminder of the importance of a free and independent press in holding those in power accountable.

In conclusion, the Duke Cunningham scandal stands as a symbol of the pervasive corruption that has plagued the highest levels of the U.S. government throughout history. It serves as a stark reminder of the need for constant vigilance and reforms to ensure transparency and accountability within our political system. Only by learning from the mistakes of the past can we hope to build a more just and ethical government for future generations.

The Ted Stevens Case: Prosecutorial Misconduct and Political Corruption

In the annals of political scandals and corruption, few cases have been as shocking and emblematic of the systemic issues plaguing the highest levels of the U.S. government as the Ted Stevens case. This infamous episode not only exposed prosecutorial misconduct but also shed light on the deep-seated political corruption that has tarnished the early years of the U.S. government.

Ted Stevens, a Republican senator from Alaska, was a powerful figure known for his influence and relentless pursuit of earmarks for his state. However, his career took a dramatic turn when he was indicted on corruption charges in 2008. The case alleged that Stevens had accepted illegal gifts and failed to disclose them on his financial disclosure forms. It seemed like a classic example of a corrupt politician caught red-handed.

However, as the case unfolded, it became apparent that the prosecution had engaged in egregious misconduct. The trial was marred by the concealment of exculpatory evidence, the manipulation of witnesses, and the withholding of evidence that could have exonerated Stevens. It was a shocking display of abuse of power and a grave violation of the principles of justice.

The Stevens case not only exposed prosecutorial misconduct but also highlighted the influence of money and lobbying in government corruption. It raised questions about the integrity of the justice system and the extent to which political pressure can sway the outcome of a trial. It also underscored the need for transparency and accountability within the government, particularly in the executive branch.

Moreover, the Stevens case was not an isolated incident. It was part of a broader pattern of corruption within Congress, where bribery and influence peddling have become all too common. This case served as a wake-up call, prompting further investigations into corruption within regulatory agencies, law enforcement, and the intelligence community.

The impact of campaign finance on government corruption also came to the forefront during the Stevens case. It became evident that the influx of money into politics was distorting the democratic process, allowing special interests to wield undue influence over elected officials. This raised concerns about the integrity of the electoral system and the need for campaign finance reform.

Furthermore, the media played a crucial role in uncovering the government misconduct in the Stevens case. It showcased the power of investigative journalism in holding the government accountable and exposing corruption. This episode highlighted the importance of a free and independent press in a democracy, ensuring that those in power are held to account.

The Ted Stevens case remains a stark reminder of the challenges that the U.S. government has faced throughout its history in combating corruption. It serves as a cautionary tale for historians studying corruption at the highest levels of the government. It underscores the need for constant vigilance, transparency, and a commitment to upholding the principles of justice and democracy. Only by learning from the mistakes of the past can we hope to build a more honest and accountable government for future generations.

Chapter 6: Corruption in law enforcement and the justice system

The Rampart Scandal: Police Corruption in LA

The Rampart Scandal stands as a dark chapter in the history of corruption within the law enforcement and justice system of Los Angeles. This subchapter explores the shocking revelation of police misconduct, the subsequent investigations, and the lasting impact it had on the community. Historians examining corruption at the highest levels of the U.S. government will find this case study illuminating, as it reveals the intersection of power, abuse, and the erosion of public trust in the justice system.

In the early 1990s, the Rampart Division of the Los Angeles Police Department (LAPD) became embroiled in a scandal that exposed widespread corruption, including drug dealing, planting evidence, assault, and perjury. The scandal came to light when a rogue officer, Rafael Perez, was caught stealing cocaine from an evidence locker. Perez, seeking a reduced sentence, began to provide shocking revelations about the extent of corruption within the department.

The revelations sent shockwaves through the city and led to the formation of an independent commission to investigate the Rampart Scandal. The commission found that not only was corruption prevalent, but it was also systemic, with officers engaging in criminal activities with impunity. The scandal raised serious questions about the integrity of the justice system and the excessive use of force by law enforcement officers.

The fallout from the scandal was significant. Over 100 convictions were overturned, and the city faced numerous lawsuits from victims of police misconduct. The LAPD, once seen as a symbol of law and order, had its reputation tarnished, and trust in the police among minority communities reached an all-time low.

The Rampart Scandal also highlighted the role of money and lobbying in government corruption. The scandal exposed a culture of silence and cover-up within the LAPD, where officers who tried to report misconduct were shunned or retaliated against. This culture of corruption was enabled by the influence of powerful police unions and the lack of accountability within the department.

This subchapter will delve into the investigations, the subsequent reforms within the LAPD, and the ongoing challenges in rebuilding public trust. It will also examine the broader implications of the Rampart Scandal for understanding corruption in law enforcement and the justice system. By examining this case study, historians can gain valuable insights into the complexities and consequences of corruption within the highest levels of the U.S. government.

The Silk Road Case: Corruption within the Dark Web Investigation

The Silk Road case stands as a significant chapter in the history of corruption within the dark web investigation. This subchapter delves into the intricate web of deceit, greed, and power that unfolded during this notorious case. As historians exploring corruption at the highest levels of the U.S. government, it is imperative to understand the impact of this case on the political landscape, law enforcement, and the justice system.

The Silk Road, an online marketplace infamous for illegal activities, was a breeding ground for corruption. Its founder, Ross Ulbricht, operated under the pseudonym "Dread Pirate Roberts" and facilitated the sale of drugs, counterfeit documents, and even weapons. This subchapter examines how corruption infiltrated the investigation, leading to serious implications for the justice system.

The case exposed the vulnerability of law enforcement agencies to corruption. Several agents involved in the investigation were found to have abused their power, embezzled confiscated funds, and even participated in illegal activities themselves. This subchapter sheds light on the ethical implications of such corruption, highlighting the need for systemic reforms within law enforcement agencies.

Furthermore, the case reveals the challenges of combating corruption within the dark web. The anonymous nature of online platforms makes it difficult to trace illegal activities and apprehend perpetrators. This subchapter explores the ethical dilemmas faced by investigators and the constant struggle to balance privacy and law enforcement.

Additionally, the Silk Road case showcases the role of media and journalism in uncovering government misconduct. Investigative journalists played a pivotal role in exposing the corrupt practices within the investigation. Their relentless pursuit of truth and justice serves as a reminder of the importance of a free and independent press in holding government accountable.

As historians, it is crucial to examine the Silk Road case not only as an isolated event but also as a reflection of broader issues of corruption within the U.S. government. This subchapter encourages a comprehensive exploration of corruption in various sectors, including the executive branch, Congress, regulatory agencies, and the intelligence community.

By analyzing the Silk Road case, historians can better understand the intricate dynamics of corruption, its far-reaching consequences, and the ongoing efforts to combat it. Ultimately, this subchapter serves as a reminder that corruption is an ever-present challenge that requires constant vigilance, accountability, and reform within the highest levels of the U.S. government.

The Gun Trace Task Force Scandal: Police Corruption in Baltimore

In the annals of corruption within law enforcement, few scandals have shaken the public's faith in the justice system as profoundly as the Gun Trace Task Force scandal in Baltimore. This subchapter delves into the intricate web of police corruption that unfolded in one of America's most troubled cities, shedding light on the long-lasting repercussions of this shocking case.

The Gun Trace Task Force, originally established to combat violent crime, ironically became a breeding ground for corruption and misconduct. This scandal, which came to light in 2017, revealed a group of Baltimore police officers engaged in a litany of illegal activities, from extortion and robbery to drug dealing and planting evidence. The revelations sent shockwaves through the city and raised serious questions about the integrity of the police force.

Examining the Gun Trace Task Force scandal offers invaluable insights into the broader issue of corruption within law enforcement and the justice system. Historians interested in understanding the impact of corruption on society will find this case study particularly enlightening. It highlights the dangerous consequences when those entrusted with upholding the law betray the public's trust, eroding the very foundations of justice and undermining community safety.

Moreover, this scandal prompts us to reflect on the systemic factors that enable such corruption to flourish. It raises questions about the role of police oversight, the influence of internal culture and leadership, and the need for robust mechanisms to detect and prevent corruption within law enforcement agencies.

The Gun Trace Task Force scandal also intersects with other themes explored in this book. It serves as a stark reminder of the dangers of unchecked power and the potential for corruption at the highest levels of government. The involvement of law enforcement in criminal activities highlights the complex relationship between corruption within the executive branch and the justice system.

Furthermore, this scandal underscores the vital role of investigative journalism in uncovering government misconduct. Without the relentless pursuit of truth by journalists, the Gun Trace Task Force scandal may have remained hidden, perpetuating the cycle of corruption and abuse of power.

Ultimately, the Gun Trace Task Force scandal stands as a cautionary tale, reminding us of the insidious nature of corruption and the urgent need for transparency, accountability, and reform within our police forces. As historians, it is our duty to examine these dark chapters of our history to better understand the roots of corruption and work towards a more just and accountable society.

The Black Sox Scandal: Baseball, Gambling, and Corruption in the Justice System

The Black Sox Scandal is a dark chapter in the history of American baseball that unraveled the intertwining web of corruption within the justice system. This subchapter delves into the scandal's intricate details, shedding light on the collusion between players, gamblers, and the flawed justice system of the early 20th century.

In 1919, the Chicago White Sox, a formidable baseball team, faced off against the Cincinnati Reds in the World Series. However, unbeknownst to the fans and the league, some players were entangled in a web of corruption. A group of players, led by the infamous "Shoeless" Joe Jackson, conspired with professional gamblers to intentionally lose the series in exchange for substantial financial rewards.

This scandal exposed the vulnerability of the justice system, as corrupt elements within law enforcement turned a blind eye to the illegal activities taking place. The gamblers involved in the scandal had strong connections within the criminal underworld, ensuring their protection from prosecution, while the players believed they could escape punishment due to their status as sports heroes.

However, the truth eventually came to light. Following a series of investigations and trials, it became evident that the players had indeed thrown the World Series. The scandal not only tarnished the reputation of the players involved but also shook the foundations of American baseball, leading to widespread disillusionment among fans.

The Black Sox Scandal served as a wake-up call for the justice system, forcing authorities to confront the issue of corruption within their ranks. It laid bare the dangers of unchecked gambling and highlighted the need for stricter regulations to protect the integrity of professional sports.

Moreover, this scandal sparked a broader conversation about corruption in American society, revealing how elements of organized crime could infiltrate even the most revered institutions. It prompted historians and policymakers to examine the role of money and lobbying in government corruption, exploring how the desire for financial gain can corrupt individuals and institutions at every level.

The Black Sox Scandal stands as a stark reminder of the importance of accountability and transparency in the justice system. It serves as a cautionary tale, urging us to remain vigilant against corruption and to continuously strive for a government free from the clutches of illicit influences. Only by acknowledging and learning from the mistakes of the past can we hope to build a more just and transparent future.

Chapter 7: Investigating corruption within regulatory agencies

The Enron Scandal: Regulatory Failure and Corporate Corruption

The Enron scandal is a prime example of regulatory failure and corporate corruption in the history of the United States. This subchapter will delve into the intricate details of this scandal, highlighting the various factors that contributed to its occurrence and the subsequent fallout.

Enron Corporation was once lauded as one of the most innovative and successful companies in the energy sector. However, in 2001, it came crashing down, revealing a web of deceit and corruption that had been carefully hidden behind a façade of success. This scandal not only shook the business world but also shed light on the shortcomings of regulatory agencies and the dire consequences of unchecked corporate power.

At the heart of the Enron scandal was the manipulation of financial statements and accounting practices to inflate the company's profits artificially. Enron executives, including CEO Kenneth Lay and CFO Andrew Fastow, exploited accounting loopholes and engaged in complex financial transactions to deceive investors and inflate stock prices. The company's auditors, Arthur Andersen, also turned a blind eye to these fraudulent activities, further highlighting the failures of regulatory oversight.

The Enron scandal unraveled when a whistleblower, Sherron Watkins, brought attention to the questionable accounting practices within the company. This led to investigations by regulatory bodies such as the Securities and Exchange Commission (SEC) and the Department of Justice. These investigations revealed a web of corruption that extended beyond Enron, implicating other major corporations and highlighting the pervasive nature of corporate misconduct.

The Enron scandal exposed the weaknesses in the regulatory framework that had allowed such fraudulent activities to occur. It highlighted the need for stronger oversight and enforcement of financial reporting standards. The subsequent passage of the Sarbanes-Oxley Act in 2002 aimed to address these issues by implementing stricter regulations and increasing penalties for corporate fraud.

Furthermore, the Enron scandal served as a wake-up call for the public and policymakers, prompting a reevaluation of the role of money and lobbying in government corruption. It highlighted the close ties between corporations and politicians, leading to a broader discussion on campaign finance reform and the influence of money in politics.

In conclusion, the Enron scandal stands as a stark reminder of the dangers of regulatory failure and corporate corruption. It serves as a cautionary tale for future generations and underscores the importance of robust regulations, strong oversight, and ethical corporate practices to prevent similar scandals from occurring in the future.

The Volkswagen Emissions Scandal: Deception and Regulatory Corruption

In the annals of government corruption, few scandals have rocked the automotive industry and regulatory agencies as profoundly as the Volkswagen emissions scandal. This subchapter delves into the intricate web of deception and regulatory corruption that unfolded, exposing the darker side of the automotive giant and the failures of regulatory oversight.

The scandal erupted in September 2015 when the Environmental Protection Agency (EPA) discovered that Volkswagen had installed illegal software, known as "defeat devices," in millions of its diesel vehicles. These devices manipulated emissions tests, allowing the vehicles to appear compliant with environmental regulations while emitting up to 40 times the legal limit of nitrogen oxide pollutants in real-world driving conditions.

The revelation sent shockwaves through the automotive industry and laid bare the extent of Volkswagen's deceit. The company had marketed its "clean diesel" vehicles as environmentally friendly and boasted about their low emissions, all the while knowingly deceiving regulators and consumers. This deliberate deception not only undermined public trust but also had severe environmental and public health implications.

As investigators dug deeper, they uncovered a web of regulatory corruption and organizational failures within Volkswagen. The scandal revealed that top executives had knowledge of the illegal software, implicating the highest levels of the company's leadership. Moreover, it exposed a systemic failure within regulatory agencies, as they had failed to uncover the deception for years despite conducting routine emissions tests.

The subchapter explores the implications of the scandal within the broader context of corruption at the highest levels of the U.S. government. It draws on historical examples of political scandals and corruption to shed light on the societal and institutional factors that contribute to such malfeasance.

Furthermore, it examines the role of money and lobbying in government corruption, highlighting how corporate influence can undermine regulatory efforts and accountability. The Volkswagen scandal serves as a stark reminder of the power vested in corporations and their ability to manipulate regulatory systems to serve their own interests.

Additionally, the subchapter scrutinizes corruption within regulatory agencies, emphasizing the need for robust oversight and the potential consequences when regulators fail to fulfill their responsibilities. It raises questions about the effectiveness of current regulatory structures and the measures required to prevent future scandals.

Ultimately, the Volkswagen emissions scandal serves as a cautionary tale, illustrating the detrimental effects of deception and regulatory corruption. It underscores the importance of transparency, accountability, and a vigilant society that holds both corporations and government officials to the highest ethical standards. By examining this scandal and its implications, historians and experts in government corruption can glean valuable lessons and insights to inform future efforts to combat corruption within the highest echelons of the U.S. government.

The Madoff Ponzi Scheme: SEC Oversight and Financial Corruption

The Madoff Ponzi Scheme stands as one of the most notorious financial scandals in the history of the United States. This subchapter delves into the intricate details of the scheme, the role of the Securities and Exchange Commission (SEC) in its oversight, and the widespread financial corruption that allowed it to flourish.

Bernard Madoff, a former chairman of the NASDAQ stock exchange, orchestrated a fraudulent investment scheme that defrauded thousands of investors out of billions of dollars. Madoff promised consistent high returns and employed a classic Ponzi scheme, using new investors' money to pay off older investors. Unbeknownst to his clients, Madoff was not investing their funds but simply shuffling money around, creating the illusion of success.

What is particularly alarming about this case is the negligence displayed by the SEC. Despite numerous red flags and tips from whistleblowers, the agency failed to conduct a proper investigation into Madoff's operations. This subchapter explores the reasons behind this failure, including bureaucratic inefficiencies, inadequate resources, and a lack of understanding of complex financial instruments.

The Madoff Ponzi Scheme also highlights the deep-rooted financial corruption that exists within the U.S. government. It raises questions about the influence of money and lobbying in shaping regulatory policies and the extent to which corruption seeps into the highest levels of government. By examining this case, historians gain insight into the systemic issues that contribute to government corruption and the challenges faced by regulatory agencies in combating financial fraud.

Furthermore, this subchapter investigates the impact of campaign finance on government corruption. It explores how campaign contributions from powerful individuals and corporations may compromise the integrity of politicians and influence their decision-making processes. The Madoff Ponzi Scheme serves as a stark reminder of the need for campaign finance reform and greater transparency in political financing.

Lastly, this subchapter sheds light on the role of the media in uncovering government misconduct. Journalists played a crucial role in exposing the Madoff Ponzi Scheme, bringing it to the attention of the public and holding regulatory agencies accountable. It examines the challenges faced by journalists in investigating government corruption and emphasizes the importance of a free and independent press in maintaining a healthy democracy.

In conclusion, the Madoff Ponzi Scheme serves as a powerful case study in corruption at the highest levels of the U.S. government. It exposes the shortcomings of regulatory oversight, the influence of money in politics, and the role of journalism in uncovering government misconduct. By delving into this scandal, historians gain valuable insights into the historical context of corruption and its ongoing impact on American society.

The Flint Water Crisis: Regulatory Negligence and Public Health Corruption

Introduction:

The Flint water crisis stands as a haunting reminder of the devastating consequences of regulatory negligence and public health corruption within the highest levels of the U.S. government. This subchapter delves into the multifaceted dimensions of this crisis, shedding light on the intricate web of corruption that led to irreparable harm to the residents of Flint, Michigan. By exploring the intersections of political scandals, regulatory failures, and public health misconduct, we can gain a deeper understanding of the systemic issues that perpetuate corruption within our government.

History of Corruption in the U.S. Government:

To fully comprehend the Flint water crisis, it is essential to contextualize it within the broader history of corruption in the U.S. government. From the early years of the nation's founding to recent instances of bribery and influence peddling, scandals have plagued various branches of government, including the executive branch, Congress, law enforcement, and regulatory agencies. This subchapter aims to connect the dots between past and present corruption, highlighting the recurring patterns and systemic failures that allow misconduct to persist.

The Flint Water Crisis Unveiled:

The Flint water crisis unfolded when the city, under a state-appointed emergency manager, switched its water source to the Flint River in 2014. This decision, driven by cost-cutting measures, led to the contamination of the city's water supply with lead and other toxic substances. As the crisis escalated, it became apparent that regulatory agencies, including the Environmental Protection Agency (EPA) and the Michigan

Department of Environmental Quality (MDEQ), had failed to enforce federal regulations and ensure the safety of Flint's residents.

Regulatory Negligence and Public Health Corruption:

Investigating corruption within regulatory agencies reveals a web of negligence, cover-ups, and collusion that allowed the Flint water crisis to persist. The impact of campaign finance on government corruption becomes evident as industry influence and lobbying efforts undermined public health concerns. Furthermore, the role of money and lobbying in government corruption highlights the inherent flaws in a system where monetary interests often supersede the well-being of the public.

Uncovering Government Misconduct:

The media plays a pivotal role in uncovering government misconduct, and the Flint water crisis was no exception. This subchapter explores the role of journalism in exposing the corruption and holding accountable those responsible for the crisis. Additionally, it examines the failures of the intelligence community, military, and defense industry to address corruption within their ranks, emphasizing the need for transparency and accountability in all sectors of government.

Conclusion:

The Flint water crisis serves as a stark reminder of the consequences of regulatory negligence and public health corruption within the highest levels of the U.S. government. By examining this crisis within the broader context of corruption throughout history, we can begin to address the systemic issues that perpetuate misconduct. Only through a thorough understanding of these issues can we hope to create a government that prioritizes the well-being of its citizens over personal gain and vested interests.

Chapter 8: The impact of campaign finance on government corruption

Citizens United: Money, Politics, and the Erosion of Democracy

In the subchapter titled "Citizens United: Money, Politics, and the Erosion of Democracy," we delve into one of the most controversial Supreme Court decisions in recent history and its profound impact on the American political system. The Citizens United v. Federal Election Commission ruling, handed down in 2010, has fundamentally altered the landscape of campaign finance and has had far-reaching consequences for the integrity of our democracy.

At its core, Citizens United centers around the issue of money in politics and the question of whether corporations should be granted the same free speech rights as individuals. In a 5-4 decision, the Supreme Court ruled that corporations and unions have the same First Amendment rights as individuals, effectively opening the floodgates for unlimited corporate spending on political campaigns.

The ramifications of this decision have been staggering. Critics argue that it has further tilted the balance of power towards wealthy special interest groups, allowing them to exert disproportionate influence over the political process. The influx of corporate money into campaigns has led to an arms race of fundraising, with candidates increasingly reliant on wealthy donors to finance their campaigns. This dependence on big money donors has raised concerns about the potential for corruption and the undermining of the public interest.

Furthermore, the Citizens United ruling has given rise to the creation of Super PACs (Political Action Committees) and dark money groups, which can accept unlimited contributions from corporations and individuals while remaining largely anonymous. This lack of transparency has made it even more difficult for the public to discern who is funding political campaigns and to hold elected officials accountable.

The erosion of democracy is evident in the increasing disconnect between the will of the people and the policies pursued by elected officials. Studies have shown that the preferences of average citizens hold little sway over policy outcomes, while the interests of wealthy donors have a much greater impact. This has led to a growing sense of disillusionment and distrust in the political system, as ordinary citizens feel their voices are being drowned out by the influence of moneyed interests.

In conclusion, the Citizens United decision has had a profound and detrimental effect on our democracy. It has allowed for the unchecked influence of money in politics and has further widened the gap between the rich and the rest of society. Understanding the consequences of this ruling is crucial for historians and those interested in exploring the history and impact of corruption at the highest levels of the U.S. government. Only by recognizing the corrosive effects of money in politics can we hope to restore the true essence of democracy and ensure that our government works for the benefit of all citizens.

Super PACs and Dark Money: Influence and Corruption in Elections

In the tumultuous world of American politics, the role of money and its influence on government decisions cannot be overstated. One of the most controversial aspects of this influence is the emergence of Super PACs and the dark money they bring into elections. This subchapter delves deep into the intricate web of corruption, exploring the insidious ways Super PACs and dark money manipulate and distort the democratic process.

Super PACs, or Political Action Committees, are organizations that can raise unlimited sums of money from corporations, unions, and individuals to support or oppose political candidates. While they are technically supposed to operate independently from the candidates they support, the reality is often quite different. These entities have become a breeding ground for corruption, blurring the lines between legal and illegal campaign financing.

The term "dark money" refers to undisclosed and untraceable contributions made to campaigns, often through nonprofit organizations. These contributions allow wealthy donors and special interest groups to exert their influence without public scrutiny. The result is a system where the voices of ordinary citizens are drowned out by the powerful and well-connected.

This subchapter examines the historical context of Super PACs and dark money, tracing their origins back to the early years of the U.S. government. It explores the political scandals and corruption that have plagued the nation throughout its history, shedding light on the ways money and lobbying have played a role in government misconduct.

Furthermore, it delves into specific instances of corruption within various branches of government. From presidential scandals to bribery in Congress, from corruption within law enforcement to regulatory agencies, this subchapter leaves no stone unturned. It also explores the impact of campaign finance on government corruption, highlighting the alarming influence that money has on the decision-making process.

Moreover, this subchapter examines the role of the intelligence community, military, defense industry, and media in uncovering government misconduct. It sheds light on spying and surveillance scandals, military procurement fraud, and the crucial role of journalism in exposing corruption.

Ultimately, this subchapter serves as a comprehensive exploration of the influence and corruption that Super PACs and dark money bring to elections. It provides historians and those interested in corruption at the highest levels of the U.S. government with a detailed analysis of the past and present, offering valuable insights into the need for transparency and accountability in our democratic processes.

The Koch Brothers: Billionaires, Campaign Finance, and Political Corruption

In the realm of political corruption, few names carry as much weight as the Koch Brothers. Charles and David Koch, the billionaire industrialists, have become synonymous with the influence of money in politics and the erosion of democratic principles. This subchapter explores their rise to power, their impact on campaign finance, and their alleged involvement in political corruption.

The story of the Koch Brothers begins with their father, Fred Koch, who built an oil refinery empire in the early 20th century. Charles and David inherited this vast wealth and used it to promote their libertarian ideals through a network of think tanks, advocacy groups, and political donations. Their influence grew exponentially following the Supreme Court's Citizens United decision in 2010, which allowed unlimited corporate spending on elections.

With their immense wealth, the Koch Brothers have poured millions of dollars into political campaigns, often through secretive, dark money channels. This has raised concerns about the corrosive effects of money on our democratic system, as politicians may feel indebted to the Kochs and other wealthy donors, rather than the interests of their constituents.

Furthermore, the Koch Brothers' political activities have been linked to a range of controversial policies and legislation. They have consistently fought against regulations on the fossil fuel industry, environmental protections, and workers' rights. Critics argue that their financial influence has effectively bought policy outcomes that favor their business interests, at the expense of the broader public.

The subchapter also delves into allegations of political corruption surrounding the Koch Brothers. While the brothers themselves have not been directly implicated in any criminal activity, there have been accusations of bribery, influence peddling, and undue influence over elected officials. These allegations highlight the potential dangers of unchecked campaign finance and the need for greater transparency in political donations.

By examining the Koch Brothers' role in campaign finance and their alleged involvement in political corruption, historians can gain valuable insights into the intersection of money, power, and democracy. This subchapter serves as a cautionary tale, reminding us of the ongoing challenges in safeguarding the integrity of our government and the importance of holding those in power accountable for their actions.

Campaign Finance Reform: Addressing the Root of Government Corruption

In the realm of government corruption, one cannot ignore the pervasive influence of money and lobbying. Throughout history, we have witnessed countless instances where the pursuit of financial gain has compromised the integrity of our political system. In this subchapter, we delve into the critical issue of campaign finance and its impact on government corruption.

From the early days of the U.S. government, political scandals and corruption have plagued our nation. However, the role of money and lobbying has been a constant thread linking these transgressions. It is crucial for historians and those interested in corruption at the highest levels of the U.S. government to understand the deep-rooted connection between campaign finance and governmental misconduct.

One of the primary reasons campaign finance reform is necessary is the potential for bribery and influence peddling. When politicians rely heavily on financial contributions to fund their campaigns, it creates a system where wealthy individuals and special interest groups can exert undue influence over policy decisions. This undermines the democratic process and fosters a culture of corruption.

Furthermore, corruption within the executive branch, such as presidential scandals, often stems from the influence of campaign financing. By examining historical cases, we can see how large campaign contributions have led to favoritism, cronyism, and even illegal activities. Similarly, corruption within Congress, particularly bribery and influence peddling, can be traced back to the sway of money in elections and campaigns.

However, it is not just the elected officials who are susceptible to the corrupting influence of campaign finance. The justice system, regulatory agencies, the intelligence community, the military, and even the media have all been affected. Investigating corruption within these institutions reveals the intricate web of financial interests that perpetuate government misconduct.

To combat this systemic issue, campaign finance reform is crucial. Implementing stricter regulations on political donations, curbing the influence of lobbying, and promoting transparency in campaign financing can help restore trust in our government. By addressing the root causes of corruption, we can strive towards a more accountable and ethical political system.

In conclusion, the impact of campaign finance on government corruption cannot be underestimated. Historians and those interested in corruption at the highest levels of the U.S. government must recognize the vital role money and lobbying play in fostering misconduct. By exploring the relationship between campaign finance and corruption, we can pave the way for meaningful reform and ensure the integrity of our democratic processes.

Chapter 9: Corruption in the intelligence community: spying and surveillance scandals

COINTELPRO: Government Surveillance and Political Repression

The subchapter on COINTELPRO in "Unveiling the Shadows: Corruption at the Highest Levels of the U.S. Government Throughout History" delves into the disturbing history of government surveillance and political repression in the United States. This chapter aims to shed light on the covert operations conducted by the Federal Bureau of Investigation (FBI) and other intelligence agencies, which targeted individuals and organizations deemed subversive or a threat to the status quo.

COINTELPRO, an acronym for Counterintelligence Program, was established by the FBI in 1956 with the purported goal of protecting national security. However, as historians have uncovered, it quickly devolved into a tool of political repression and abuse of power. Under the guise of maintaining law and order, COINTELPRO engaged in illegal activities such as wiretapping, infiltration, and the dissemination of disinformation to disrupt and neutralize various political movements.

One of the primary targets of COINTELPRO was the civil rights movement, particularly its leaders such as Martin Luther King Jr. and the Black Panther Party. The FBI, under the leadership of J. Edgar Hoover, viewed these groups as threats to the existing power structure and used every means at their disposal to undermine their efforts. This included sowing discord within the organizations, fabricating evidence, and even resorting to violence.

Furthermore, COINTELPRO extended its reach to other political movements such as anti-war activists, feminist groups, and Native

American organizations. The surveillance and harassment tactics employed by the government infringed upon the constitutional rights of countless individuals who were merely exercising their First Amendment rights to free speech and assembly.

This subchapter also explores the impact of COINTELPRO on the broader landscape of government corruption. It raises important questions about the role of intelligence agencies, the erosion of civil liberties, and the abuse of power by those in positions of authority. By examining the tactics and consequences of COINTELPRO, historians can gain a deeper understanding of the dangers posed by unchecked government surveillance and the implications for democracy.

In conclusion, the subchapter on COINTELPRO in "Unveiling the Shadows: Corruption at the Highest Levels of the U.S. Government Throughout History" provides a comprehensive analysis of government surveillance and political repression. It highlights the abuses of power committed in the name of national security, and the lasting impact of these actions on American society. By studying this dark chapter in our history, historians can contribute to a broader understanding of corruption and the need for transparency and accountability in our government institutions.

NSA Wiretapping Scandal: Government Surveillance and Privacy Rights

In the age of digital communication and advanced technology, the issue of government surveillance and privacy rights has become increasingly important. One scandal that has brought this issue to the forefront is the NSA wiretapping scandal. This subchapter will delve into the details of this scandal, examining its implications for corruption at the highest levels of the U.S. government throughout history.

The NSA wiretapping scandal refers to the revelation that the National Security Agency had been secretly collecting and monitoring the communications of American citizens without their knowledge or consent. This widespread surveillance program, known as PRISM, came to light in 2013 when whistleblower Edward Snowden leaked classified documents to the media. The revelations shocked the nation and sparked a fierce debate about the balance between national security and individual privacy rights.

Historians studying corruption at the highest levels of the U.S. government will find the NSA wiretapping scandal particularly intriguing as it highlights the abuse of power by intelligence agencies. This scandal is not an isolated incident but rather part of a historical pattern of government overreach and intrusion into the private lives of its citizens.

Examining the NSA wiretapping scandal also offers insights into the role of money and lobbying in government corruption. The vast resources allocated to intelligence agencies enable them to carry out surveillance programs without proper oversight, thus undermining the checks and balances that are essential for a transparent and accountable government.

Furthermore, this scandal raises questions about corruption in the intelligence community and the military-industrial complex. The NSA's collaboration with telecommunications companies and its close ties to defense contractors shed light on the potential for corruption within these sectors.

Privacy rights have long been a contentious issue, and the NSA wiretapping scandal serves as a powerful case study highlighting the tension between national security and individual liberties. It underscores the need for robust legal and regulatory frameworks to protect citizens' privacy rights and prevent government overreach.

Ultimately, the NSA wiretapping scandal is an important chapter in the history of corruption at the highest levels of the U.S. government. Its ramifications extend beyond the intelligence community, shedding light on broader issues of government misconduct, the influence of money in politics, and the role of journalism in uncovering such scandals. By studying this scandal, historians can gain valuable insights into the challenges of maintaining a transparent and accountable government in an increasingly complex and interconnected world.

Edward Snowden and the NSA Leaks: Whistleblowing and Government Misconduct

The revelations brought forth by Edward Snowden in 2013 regarding the National Security Agency's (NSA) widespread surveillance and data collection practices sent shockwaves throughout the world. Snowden, a former NSA contractor, blew the whistle on the agency's unconstitutional activities, exposing the government's misconduct and violating the privacy rights of millions of individuals. This subchapter delves into the significance of this event in the context of corruption at the highest levels of the U.S. government.

Whistleblowing has long played a crucial role in uncovering government misconduct, and Snowden's actions were no exception. By leaking classified documents, he provided irrefutable evidence of the NSA's excessive surveillance programs, including the mass collection of phone records and internet communications. These revelations sparked a global conversation about the balance between national security and individual privacy rights, ultimately leading to significant reforms in surveillance practices.

Snowden's actions also shed light on the inherent corruption within the intelligence community. The NSA's overreach demonstrated a lack of accountability and transparency, raising questions about the oversight mechanisms in place to prevent such abuses of power. This subchapter explores the implications of unchecked government surveillance and the potential for abuse of authority within the intelligence community.

Furthermore, the Snowden leaks exposed the close relationship between the government and technology companies, highlighting the role of money and lobbying in government corruption. It became evident that major tech corporations were complicit in the NSA's surveillance programs, raising concerns about the influence of money and corporate interests on government policies and practices.

The impact of whistleblowing on public perception and government accountability is a central theme in this subchapter. Snowden's actions ignited debates on the balance between national security and civil liberties, forcing the government to confront the issue of government surveillance head-on. This chapter also examines the role of journalism in uncovering government misconduct, as journalists played a vital role in reporting on the Snowden leaks and exposing the extent of the NSA's activities.

In conclusion, Edward Snowden's whistleblowing on the NSA's surveillance practices was a pivotal moment in the history of government corruption in the United States. His actions raised important questions about the limits of government power, the role of money and lobbying in corruption, and the need for robust oversight mechanisms. By exploring the implications of the Snowden leaks, this subchapter sheds light on the ongoing challenges of combating corruption at the highest levels of the U.S. government.

The CIA Torture Scandal: Human Rights Abuses and Government Corruption

In the annals of U.S. government corruption, few chapters are as disturbing and morally bankrupt as the CIA Torture Scandal. This dark episode in American history revealed the depths to which our government was willing to sink in its pursuit of national security, at the cost of human rights and the principles upon which our nation was built.

The scandal emerged in the early 2000s, following the 9/11 terrorist attacks that shook the nation. In the wake of this tragedy, the CIA, under the guise of preserving national security, engaged in a program of enhanced interrogation techniques, which many have since labeled as torture. These techniques included waterboarding, sleep deprivation, stress positions, and other forms of physical and psychological abuse.

At the heart of this scandal was the erosion of human rights. The United States, a nation built on the principles of liberty and justice, had stooped to violating the very values it purported to uphold. The actions of the CIA not only violated international laws and treaties, but also the basic principles of human decency. This scandal revealed a government willing to sacrifice its moral compass in the name of security.

Furthermore, the CIA Torture Scandal exposed the extent of government corruption at the highest levels. It was not just the actions of a few rogue agents, but a systematic and coordinated effort that reached the upper echelons of power. The leaders and policymakers who authorized and condoned these practices were complicit in the erosion of our values and the betrayal of the American people's trust.

The scandal also highlighted the need for accountability and transparency in our government. The cover-up and denial that followed the revelation of these abuses demonstrated a government unwilling to confront its own misdeeds. It took the courage of whistleblowers and investigative journalists to bring this scandal to light, underscoring the crucial role of the media in exposing government misconduct.

As historians, it is our duty to examine and learn from the mistakes of the past. The CIA Torture Scandal serves as a stark reminder of the dangers of unchecked power and the corrosive effects of government corruption.

It is a call to action for all Americans to demand transparency, accountability, and adherence to the principles that define our democracy.

In the pages that follow, we will delve deeper into the CIA Torture Scandal, exploring its origins, the individuals involved, and the impact it had on our nation. By shining a light on this dark chapter in our history, we hope to contribute to the ongoing dialogue on corruption at the highest levels of the U.S. government and inspire a renewed commitment to upholding our core values.

Chapter 10: Examining corruption in the military and defense industry

The Military-Industrial Complex: Corruption and Profiteering

In the subchapter titled "The Military-Industrial Complex: Corruption and Profiteering," we delve into one of the most pervasive and enduring forms of corruption at the highest levels of the U.S. government. Throughout history, the military-industrial complex has played a significant role in shaping American politics and policy, often at the expense of transparency, accountability, and ethical conduct.

From its inception, the military-industrial complex has been plagued by corruption and profiteering. In the early years of the U.S. government, political scandals and corruption were rife, and the defense industry was not immune. Contractors and suppliers capitalized on their close ties to government officials, using bribery and influence peddling to secure lucrative contracts and favorable treatment.

The role of money and lobbying in government corruption cannot be understated. Over the years, defense contractors and their lobbyists have wielded immense influence, using campaign contributions and other forms of financial support to sway policymakers and ensure their interests are protected. This unholy alliance between moneyed interests and politicians has eroded the democratic process and perpetuated a system of cronyism and favoritism.

Corruption within the military-industrial complex is not limited to contractors alone. Presidential scandals have revealed instances of high-ranking officials using their positions for personal gain or to benefit their friends and allies. Congress, too, has been implicated in bribery and influence peddling, with lawmakers often succumbing to the allure of financial rewards in exchange for their support on defense-related matters.

Moreover, corruption within regulatory agencies tasked with overseeing the defense industry has further facilitated the growth of this shadowy network. Instances of officials turning a blind eye to violations and irregularities have allowed unscrupulous actors to continue profiting at the expense of taxpayers.

The impact of campaign finance on government corruption cannot be ignored. The influx of money into political campaigns has created a system where politicians are beholden to their deep-pocketed donors, compromising the integrity of the decision-making process and fostering an environment ripe for corruption within the military-industrial complex.

Examining corruption within the military and defense industry is essential to understanding the extent of misconduct and its consequences for national security and public trust. From spying and surveillance scandals within the intelligence community to the manipulation of contracts and the exploitation of loopholes, the rot of corruption has permeated every aspect of this powerful sector.

Uncovering government misconduct within the military-industrial complex requires a vigilant and independent media. Journalists play a crucial role in shedding light on malfeasance, holding public officials accountable, and ultimately safeguarding the democratic principles upon which this nation was founded.

In conclusion, the military-industrial complex has long been a hotbed of corruption and profiteering. From the early years of the U.S. government to the present day, the intertwining of money, power, and politics has fueled a culture of unethical behavior and undermined the very foundations of our democracy. By understanding the historical context and exploring the intricate web of corruption within this sector, we can work towards a more transparent and accountable government that prioritizes the interests of the people over those of a privileged few.

The Pentagon Papers: Government Deception and Corruption in the Vietnam War

In the subchapter titled "The Pentagon Papers: Government Deception and Corruption in the Vietnam War," we delve into one of the most significant instances of government deceit and corruption in American history. The release of the Pentagon Papers exposed a web of lies and manipulation at the highest levels of the U.S. government during the Vietnam War. This chapter sheds light on this dark chapter in our nation's history, providing historians with a comprehensive analysis of the events that unfolded.

The Vietnam War was a deeply divisive conflict that claimed the lives of thousands of American soldiers and countless Vietnamese civilians. However, what the American public did not know at the time was the extent to which the government had misled them about the true nature and progress of the war. The Pentagon Papers, leaked by military analyst Daniel Ellsberg in 1971, revealed a shocking series of deceptions perpetuated by the government.

The papers exposed how successive administrations had systematically lied to the American people about the progress of the war, the true intentions behind U.S. involvement, and the extent of civilian casualties. They also revealed the extent of corruption and profiteering within the military-industrial complex, with defense contractors exploiting the war for personal gain.

Furthermore, the Pentagon Papers highlighted the role of money and lobbying in government corruption. It became clear that powerful interests had influenced policy decisions, perpetuating a war that was not only morally questionable but also financially beneficial to a select few. The influence of money in government decision-making processes came under scrutiny, raising concerns about the integrity of the democratic system.

This subchapter also explores the impact of the Pentagon Papers on the media and the role of journalism in uncovering government misconduct. The release of these classified documents sparked a nationwide debate about the role of the media in holding the government accountable. It demonstrated the power of investigative journalism in exposing corruption and prompted a reevaluation of the relationship between the press and the government.

By examining the Pentagon Papers, historians gain valuable insight into the extent of corruption and deception within the U.S. government during the Vietnam War. It serves as a cautionary tale, reminding us of the importance of transparency, accountability, and ethical governance. The lessons learned from this dark period in our history can inform our understanding of corruption at the highest levels of the U.S. government and inspire us to demand better from our leaders.

The Halliburton Scandal: Corruption, War Profits, and Government Contracts

In the annals of American political scandals, few are as notorious as the Halliburton scandal. This chapter delves into the web of corruption, war profits, and government contracts that surrounded this infamous episode. By examining the Halliburton scandal, we gain a deeper understanding of the insidious nature of corruption at the highest levels of the U.S. government.

The story begins with the Iraq War, a conflict shrouded in controversy from its inception. As the war unfolded, Halliburton, an energy services company, emerged as a major player in the military-industrial complex.

Led by its former CEO, Dick Cheney, who also served as Vice President under President George W. Bush, Halliburton secured lucrative government contracts for reconstruction efforts in Iraq.

However, what appeared to be a legitimate business arrangement soon unraveled into a cesspool of corruption. It was revealed that Halliburton had overcharged the government for its services, engaged in bid-rigging, and even provided subpar workmanship. This scandal exposed the dark underbelly of government contracting, where profits often trumped accountability and transparency.

The Halliburton scandal also highlighted the role of money and lobbying in government corruption. Halliburton had a long history of cozy relationships with politicians, leveraging their connections and financial contributions to secure lucrative contracts. This chapter explores how the nexus of money, politics, and influence peddling perpetuates corruption within the executive branch and Congress.

Furthermore, the impact of campaign finance on government corruption is examined through the lens of the Halliburton scandal. The case demonstrates how the flood of money into political campaigns can create a system of quid pro quo, where politicians are beholden to their wealthy donors rather than the interests of the public.

Additionally, this chapter uncovers the role of the media in exposing government misconduct. Investigative journalists played a crucial role in uncovering the Halliburton scandal, shining a light on the corrupt practices that had been perpetrated for years. Their work serves as a reminder of the vital role that journalism plays in holding the government accountable.

Ultimately, the Halliburton scandal serves as a cautionary tale, revealing the pervasive nature of corruption in the highest echelons of power. By examining this dark chapter in our history, historians gain valuable insights into the mechanisms of government corruption and the urgent need for transparency and ethical governance.

The Abu Ghraib Scandal: Military Misconduct and Government Accountability

The Abu Ghraib scandal stands as one of the most notorious cases of military misconduct and government accountability in recent history. This subchapter delves into the shocking events that unfolded at the Abu Ghraib prison in Iraq, shedding light on the systemic corruption that allowed such atrocities to occur. By examining this scandal, historians can gain a deeper understanding of the dark underbelly of the U.S. government and its implications on military operations and international relations.

The Abu Ghraib scandal erupted in 2003 when disturbing photographs emerged, showcasing the brutal mistreatment and torture of Iraqi prisoners by American soldiers. These images captured the attention of the world, revealing a shocking abuse of power and a complete disregard for human rights. As historians, it is essential to dissect the factors that contributed to this scandal and to hold the government accountable for its failures.

One key aspect to explore is the role of military misconduct within a broader context of corruption. The Abu Ghraib scandal exposes how a culture of impunity can thrive within the military, allowing for the abuse of power and the erosion of ethical standards. By examining this case, historians can shed light on the need for robust accountability measures within the military and defense industry.

Furthermore, the subchapter delves into the issue of government accountability. The scandal at Abu Ghraib raises important questions about the responsibility of government officials in overseeing military operations and ensuring the protection of human rights. By analyzing the failures in leadership and oversight that allowed this scandal to occur, historians can provide valuable insights into the need for stronger governmental checks and balances.

Ultimately, the Abu Ghraib scandal serves as a stark reminder of the potential for corruption and misconduct within the U.S. government. By examining this dark chapter in history, historians can contribute to a deeper understanding of corruption at the highest levels of the U.S. government. This subchapter offers a comprehensive analysis of the Abu Ghraib scandal, shedding light on the need for transparency, accountability, and ethical governance in order to prevent similar atrocities from occurring in the future.

Chapter 11: Corruption and the media: exploring the role of journalism in uncovering government misconduct

Watergate and the Role of Investigative Journalism

The Watergate scandal is undoubtedly one of the most infamous events in American political history. It not only led to the resignation of President Richard Nixon but also exposed a web of corruption at the highest levels of the U.S. government. This subchapter delves into the significance of investigative journalism in uncovering and unraveling the Watergate scandal, highlighting its role in exposing government misconduct.

Investigative journalism played a pivotal role in bringing the Watergate scandal to light. Reporters Bob Woodward and Carl Bernstein of The Washington Post pursued a relentless investigation, relying on anonymous sources and leaked documents. Their groundbreaking reporting revealed a complex web of illegal activities, including the break-in at the Democratic National Committee headquarters, illegal wiretapping, and a vast cover-up orchestrated by the Nixon administration.

Woodward and Bernstein's reporting not only exposed the wrongdoings but also fostered public outrage and led to extensive investigations by Congress and the judiciary. Their work highlighted the crucial role of the media as the fourth estate, acting as a watchdog over the government and holding those in power accountable.

The Watergate scandal marked a turning point in American journalism, as it showcased the power of investigative reporting to bring about significant political change. It inspired a new generation of journalists, encouraging them to dig deeper and challenge the official narrative. The scandal also led to reforms in journalism practices, emphasizing the importance of fact-checking, verification, and ethical reporting.

Furthermore, the Watergate scandal demonstrated the necessity of a free and independent press in a democracy. It showcased the media's ability to act as a check on government power, ensuring transparency and accountability. The scandal also highlighted the risks journalists face when exposing government corruption, such as threats, intimidation, and legal battles.

Today, as we reflect on the Watergate scandal, it serves as a reminder of the essential role investigative journalism plays in our society. It underscores the need for journalists to remain dedicated to uncovering the truth, even in the face of adversity. The legacy of Watergate continues to inspire journalists to expose corruption, holding our government accountable and ensuring the integrity of our democracy.

In conclusion, the Watergate scandal and the role of investigative journalism in uncovering government misconduct are of paramount importance in understanding the history of corruption at the highest levels of the U.S. government. This subchapter sheds light on the significance of the scandal, the impact of investigative reporting, and the enduring lessons it holds for both historians and those interested in exploring corruption within the government.

The Panama Papers: Exposing Global Corruption through Journalism

In the subchapter, "The Panama Papers: Exposing Global Corruption through Journalism," we delve into one of the most significant and far-reaching revelations of corruption in recent history. The Panama Papers leak, which occurred in 2016, exposed the hidden wealth and illicit financial activities of countless politicians, businessmen, and celebrities around the world. This unprecedented leak was made possible by a collaboration between an anonymous whistleblower and a team of investigative journalists from the International Consortium of Investigative Journalists (ICIJ).

The Panama Papers leak shed light on the dark underbelly of global corruption, revealing a complex web of offshore accounts, shell companies, and money laundering schemes. The leaked documents, originating from the Panama-based law firm Mossack Fonseca, implicated high-ranking officials from countries across the globe, including some within the United States government.

For historians interested in corruption at the highest levels of the U.S. government, the Panama Papers provide valuable insights into the role of money and lobbying in government corruption. The leaked documents exposed how politicians and influential individuals used offshore accounts to hide their wealth and evade taxes, giving them undue influence over the political process.

Furthermore, the Panama Papers revealed the extent of corruption within the executive branch, as several world leaders, including some U.S. allies, were implicated in the scandal. This subchapter investigates presidential scandals and the various forms of corruption that have plagued the highest office in the land throughout history.

Additionally, the Panama Papers shed light on corruption within Congress, exposing instances of bribery and influence peddling. These revelations prompt an examination of the relationship between money, lobbying, and government corruption, providing historians with a deeper understanding of the challenges faced by the U.S. political system.

Furthermore, the role of journalism in uncovering government misconduct cannot be overstated. The Panama Papers leak exemplifies the power of investigative journalism in holding those in power accountable. This subchapter explores the impact of the media's role in exposing government corruption and the challenges faced by journalists in conducting such investigations.

In conclusion, the Panama Papers leak stands as a monumental moment in the fight against corruption. By uncovering the hidden wealth and illicit activities of global elites, this leak brought to light the extent of corruption within governments worldwide, including the highest levels of the U.S. government. For historians interested in corruption at the highest levels of the U.S. government and the role of journalism in exposing government misconduct, the Panama Papers provide a wealth of information and insights.

The Snowden Revelations: Journalistic Ethics and Government Secrets

In the digital age, where information is readily accessible and the lines between privacy and national security are blurred, the Snowden revelations have raised important questions about journalistic ethics and government secrets. Edward Snowden, a former NSA contractor, shocked the world in 2013 when he leaked classified documents that exposed the extent of government surveillance programs.

For historians studying corruption at the highest levels of the U.S. government, the Snowden revelations offer a unique lens into the inner workings of power. By examining the ethical considerations that journalists faced when reporting on these government secrets, we can gain a deeper understanding of the challenges and responsibilities they encounter when uncovering government misconduct.

Journalists are tasked with the responsibility of informing the public while also abiding by ethical principles, such as minimizing harm and ensuring accuracy. However, in cases like the Snowden revelations, where the information being leaked is of immense public interest, navigating these ethical waters becomes increasingly complex.

One of the key ethical dilemmas faced by journalists in the aftermath of the Snowden revelations was the balance between national security and the right to privacy. By exposing the extent of government surveillance programs, journalists were forced to confront the potential harm caused by these programs. On one hand, the public had a right to know about the violation of their privacy. On the other hand, the release of classified information could potentially compromise national security.

Additionally, journalists had to grapple with the legal implications of publishing classified information. The U.S. government argued that the leaked documents jeopardized national security and violated the Espionage Act. Journalists had to weigh the potential legal consequences against the public interest in being informed about the government's actions. Ultimately, these ethical decisions shaped the way the Snowden revelations were reported and how the public perceived the government's actions.

The impact of the Snowden revelations extended beyond the realm of journalism ethics. It ignited a broader conversation about government transparency, accountability, and the balance between security and privacy. It also shed light on the role of whistleblowers in exposing government misconduct and the need for legal protections to encourage transparency.

As historians, it is crucial to examine the Snowden revelations within the larger context of corruption at the highest levels of the U.S. government. By studying the ethical considerations faced by journalists and the implications of government secrecy, we can gain a deeper understanding of the challenges that have persisted throughout history. Moreover, we can explore how these revelations have shaped public opinion, influenced policy decisions, and paved the way for future reforms in government transparency and accountability.

Investigative Reporting in the Digital Age: Challenges and Opportunities for Uncovering Government Corruption

In the digital age, investigative reporting has emerged as a powerful tool to uncover government corruption and hold those in power accountable. The increased accessibility and speed of information provided by the internet and digital technologies have revolutionized the way journalists approach their work. This subchapter explores the challenges and opportunities faced by investigative reporters in their mission to unveil government corruption, with a focus on the highest levels of the U.S. government throughout history.

One of the greatest challenges faced by investigative journalists is the sheer complexity of the subject matter. Government corruption is often deeply entrenched, involving intricate networks of power and influence. However, the digital age has empowered journalists with an array of tools to navigate this complexity. Data mining, social media analysis, and online research have become essential skills for investigative reporters, allowing them to uncover patterns of corruption and connect the dots like never before.

Moreover, the digital age has also provided opportunities for collaboration and information sharing among journalists. Investigative reporting is no longer limited to a single newsroom or publication. Through online platforms and networks, reporters can work together, pooling their resources and expertise to tackle complex investigations that would have been impossible to undertake alone. This collaborative approach has proven particularly effective in exposing government corruption, as it allows for a broader perspective and a more comprehensive analysis of the issue at hand.

However, the digital age also presents challenges that must be addressed. The rise of fake news and misinformation poses a significant threat to the credibility of investigative reporting. Journalists must be vigilant in verifying information and sources, as well as educating the public on how to discern reliable news from falsehoods.

Additionally, the increasing sophistication of surveillance technologies poses ethical questions for investigative reporters. While these technologies can provide valuable evidence in uncovering corruption, they also raise concerns about privacy and the potential for abuse. Journalists must navigate this ethical minefield carefully, ensuring that their investigative methods align with ethical standards and do not infringe upon individuals' rights.

In conclusion, investigative reporting in the digital age has both challenges and opportunities for uncovering government corruption. The complexity of the subject matter necessitates the use of digital tools and collaboration among journalists. However, journalists must also grapple with the threats posed by fake news and surveillance technologies. By navigating these challenges, investigative reporters can continue to play a crucial role in exposing government misconduct and upholding the principles of transparency and accountability.